Acing the South African Music Industry

BY

Colani "SooPurB" Nkosi

Acing the South African Music Industry

Disclaimer

The Publishers and Editors cannot be held responsible for errors or any consequences arising from the use of information contained in this book; the views and opinions expressed do not necessarily reflect those of Mbokodo Publishers, its affiliates, or its employees, neither does the publication of this book constitute any endorsement by the Publishers and Editors of the views expressed herein.

Publisher's Competency

Licensed Educator (SACE), Bachelor of Administration in Public Management (University of Pretoria), Licentiate in Ministerial Theology (PBC), Certified Editor (College SA), English for Language Practitioners (University of Pretoria), Publishing studies (University of Pretoria). Commissioner of Oaths and Marriage Officer (SA). In progress: Bachelor of Laws (UNISA).

ACING THE SOUTH AFRICAN MUSIC INDUSTRY ISBN-13: 978-1-990919-82-4 (paperback)

ISBN-13: 978-1-990919-83-1 (pdf) ISBN-13: 978-1-990919-84-8 (ebook)

Published by

Typeset in 10/11 Garamond by Mbokodo Publishers Printed by Mbokodo Publishers 1 2 3 4 5 1 2

Every effort has been made to obtain copyright permission for the material used in this book. Please contact the Author with any queries in this regard.

Colani "SooPurB"

ABOUT THE AUTHOR

I'm Colani Nkosi (born 16 April 1994) known in the music business as SooPurB. I'm a rapper, singer, songwriter, and record producer hailing from Mpumalanga, Nhlazatshe. I spent almost all my life in this neighbourhood. I got my pre-school, primary, and high school education in Nhlazatshe public schools. My parents couldn't afford private institutions. My mom has been a farm and domestic worker her whole life and my dad worked in a butchery and he passed away a few years after he started working at a mine. After passing matric in 2012 with a bachelor's endorsement, the following year, 2013 I went to study my three-year communication studies degree at the University of Limpopo and completed it on record time, 2015.

I've been in school since I was young, I only got to be home and chill in 2016 though I was stressed by job hunting. Since December 2015 I started sending out CVs applying for jobs and internships. Welcome to South Africa where only a few professions offer permanent employment to people coming straight out of tertiary, like the education sector, where no experience is required. In other professions, they require 3 years or more of experience and worse internships are only one-year contracts and a person can't do more than one. it's a mess.

I've been in and out of offices doing internship interviews mostly in Gauteng and none of those came to fruition. In December 2016, I got a call inviting me to an interview in my home city Mbombela. It was an internship (Radio Content Production) interview at SABC, Ligwalagwala FM and I succeeded.

Because Nhlazatshe is a bit far from the SABC Mbombela offices/studios, I had to relocate to a township that is closer to the workplace. I rented a room in Barberton, a place that's 40km away from Mbombela and I relied on Buscor buses which are offering affordable transportation to the city and back daily.

Colani "SooPurB"

Monday to Friday, 8 am to 4 pm, I was at SABC doing content production, scriptwriting, translating, audio recording and editing, stakeholder liaising, website and social media content creation and management. In February I was familiar with almost all the duties and tools used so I began enjoying my experiential work. And to tell you the truth, in any radio station, be it local, commercial or national, the busiest and fastest of all shows, is the breakfast show.

Being part of the breakfast show team was a blessing and a half for several reasons. I learned to work under pressure because of the show's fast- paced setup. My mentor who also happened to be the producer of the show, Mr Sehlabela aka BeKay has been on the radio for years producing and presenting and during my internship, he was acting as the station's programmes manager so he got a lot of experience and I gained a lot from him. He showed me how to do things once and let me do the work on my own. He just let me learn by doing, making mistakes, and most importantly learn from them.

I was also warmly welcomed by the hosts of the show, Dj Madumane and Mpumi Mbethe (who later left to join Rise FM). And the sports and news presenters were cool except one old lady, a veteran newsreader, who always thought I'm the one who tempered with the news soundbites desktop if it wasn't functional or the chair got misplaced. Nonetheless, I was working well with most people from various departments in the building.

The minute I started dealing and liaising with artists and their managers, both well-known and upcoming, I learned the "DOs and DON'Ts" of requesting and securing radio interviews. I also got to know why other artists succeed in getting interviews and why others fail. I got to learn how PR specialists send music to radio stations. I also got to see how artist management and public relations practitioners of big artists operate, how they write their emails, and what they specifically attach. I was there to learn and gain experience in radio programming but as an aspiring artist, I was subtly studying the music business in the process.

Whenever artists requested interviews, I was the one scheduling and confirming for the breakfast show and my mentor was supervising. When we hosted an artist, my duty was to welcome them, making sure their song is scheduled by the music compiler and making sure that everyone is on the same page. I was also lucky that Mpumi Mbethe (having worked on national TV, both behind the scenes and on-screen) was co-hosting the show and

I learned a lot about the media and entertainment industry from her. One thing you should know about her is that she always carries a book to read with her wherever she goes, you'll always find a book or two in her car or her handbag. She reads like crazy and as a result, she stays too damn smart.

I must say that I was lucky and blessed to be an intern at Ligwalagwala FM and especially in the programming department because that's where the music business meets radio. Having the privilege to see how successful artists and prominent record labels interacted with radio, put me in the position to learn the exact ways of submitting music to radio and what other materials and details are supposed to come along with a song for it to be played. And I also learned the exact requirements and radio standards that an artist and their music have to meet.

INTRODUCTION

At the beginning of the year 2020, during recording my debut EP titled KWASUKASUKELA, the idea of writing a music business self-help book persistently occurred in my mind and I finally succumbed to it and began to write the manuscript. The idea came from my will and desire to share the little knowledge I have acquired in the past few years of chasing my dream as an aspiring music artist. I decided to share the ups and downs I came across, mistakes I made, and most importantly the lessons I've learned.

My passion for music began when I was in primary school. Whenever a hot song was dominating the airwaves and buzzing in the streets, I'd write my version and try to come up with lyrics and a tune of my own. My elder brothers used to play a lot of RnB and Kwatio, but because I couldn't sing properly I knew from the beginning that RnB isn't the genre for me to focus on. I still love and listen to RnB and other genres but Hip Hop possessed me. I guess I was also hooked by the lifestyle of successful Hip Hop artists.

Back then the SA Hip Hop scene was run by the likes of Skwatta Kamp, Tuks Senganga, Khuli Chana, Morafe, Teargas, Jozi, Amu, the late Linda "Pro" Mkhize was rocking Mzansi with hits such as 'Move,' 'Bumpa,' and the late Jabulani "HHP" Tsambo was serving us hits such as 'Tswaka,' 'Music and Lights,' and more. As much as Hip Hop has been my daily starter, main course, and desert, I've always listened to and enjoyed other types of music, both international and local.

In 2008, my first year in high school I met and befriended a Hip-Hop/Rap fanatic by the name of Xolani Ndlovu and we happened to be classmates. That dude was a Rap/Hip Hop addict and most people in school used to call him 'M'rapper.' He was always reciting known and unknown Rap/Hop- Hop songs by South African and American rappers. In the USA, the Hip Hop game was led by Lil Wayne, introducing us to the likes of Drake, Niki Minaj, and the whole Young Money Squad.

In Mzansi, Ghetto Ruff, now Muthaland Entertainment was home to most Hip Hop artists. Xolani introduced me to a whole lot of things that have to do with Hip Hop culture, music, and lifestyle. I then started to carry a notepad in my school backpack on which I was penning my rap verses. During free periods, which we barely had, or when a teacher wasn't in class, we would write and recite our whack rhymes. And my dress code gradually changed to resemble that of my idols.

My friend and two friends of his who went to a nearby high school formed a trio and called themselves 'Musketeers' and they started recording songs in bedroom studios. I also joined forces with two of my childhood friends and we started writing and recording our songs as well. A producer from Malawi by name of Richard Kulinji owned a bedroom studio and he was our go-to guy.

Hearing ourselves on records made by us and performing on local and school functions was blissful. Being known that you rap in school and the hood was a cool thing during those days. And people who weren't part of the culture would call you a 'nigga.' Because we were young and clueless we didn't do much with our music. The school was the main thing and rapping and making music was just a hobby.

In my second year in varsity, 2014 I met a Venda producer, G-Boy who owned a bedroom studio, and with him, I recorded a mixtape consisting of 13 songs but they weren't of good quality so I shared the tape with friends and considered the whole project nothing but practice. In 2017 I started to chase my music dream with seriousness and professionalism. Of course, I knew nothing about the music business but I made a promise to myself that I'd learn by doing.

Being a one-man army doing my administration, doing my PR, and relying on myself financially has been a tough but eye-opening and learning experience for me, and with this book, I aim to share all the lessons I've learned with the hope that other aspiring artists can use the knowledge to their advantage as they pursue their music careers.

CHAPTER 1

Music Production

The term 'music production' sounds like it's music engineering jargon or

some sort of music science lingo only meant for audio engineers but hell no it's not. Music production simply means 'music-making or making music.' Of course, engineering is part of music production but the term refers to the entire creative process. Well, I'm not an English expert but all I'm trying to say is that music production is the process of making a song from the start to finish. Writing lyrics, coming up with a tune, making or composing a beat (instrumental), recording vocals, arranging, mixing, and mastering, all are elements of music production (making music).

These are not the only elements of making a song, there's more depending on the type of music made and how it's made. However, all the parts or pieces need to be in harmony with one another for the song to be worth listening to. So many people are involved in the process of making a song, ranging from a composer, beatmaker, producer, author (writer or lyricist), engineer, backing vocalists, and more. And if one of these people flop, the entire song will suck. It's therefore important to work with people who got skills.

Well, I'm not an expert on music production and I don't wanna talk about what makes a song of good quality or a radio-friendly song, I just wanna share with you the things I did and paid thorough attention to make my songs sound good and of course not get rejected on major platforms because my aim always has been to get airplay. What I did with my first two songs, 'Nkebelele & Skelem' and what I still do to ensure my music is of good quality; I CHOOSE TO WORK WITH PEOPLE WHO MADE SONGS THAT PLAYED ON RADIO BEFORE.

To have a song that will be played on the radio, work with a person who once achieved that. I chose to have my songs recorded, mixed, and mastered by Jay Spitter for one reason and one reason only, his songs made it to radio and I wanted the same thing with my songs...getting played. No matter what you want to achieve in life, get help from people who you're sure to have done that thing and have done it successfully. Well, there's no guarantee but the chances are high compared to working with amateurs.

As I worked on my debut EP, I consciously chose to have the songs mixed and mastered by someone who worked on songs that got approved on national platforms such as Channel O, Yfm, and more. When I heard 3 Steps' music for the first time I was startled by the quality and it was no surprise that one of his songs topped charts on Yfm, and its video got playlisted on a major TV channel, Channel O.

So logically if I want to hear my song playing on the radio, I must get people who make songs that get played on the radio. I also apply the same strategy when looking for people to do other services for me. For instance, if I want to see my music video playing on a major television channel, I must get someone who shot videos that play on TV to shoot a music video for me.

The minute I decided to take my passion seriously, I made a promise to myself that I will never and never again work with anybody for the sake of just getting the work done. Before I work with or hire a person I first check their work and track record (a summary of their accomplishments) the same way companies check CVs before employing workers. Why would I ask a direction to Canine from someone who didn't even make it out of Egypt? It's unlikely that a person who has never set their foot and eyes in a place will be able to give give you proper directions to that place.

Most of us as artists simply can't judge a song's quality, it's not our field and just because you can hear the vocals and the beat going together, it doesn't mean a song is of good quality. It takes an experienced audio engineer's ear, skills, and to determine whether a song is of high quality. Work with a person who's done the job successfully, don't go for anyone and cheap prices. You must start investing in your craft from the very beginning.

Another important thing to take into consideration before writing a song, selecting a beat, and deciding on the overall sound is relevancy. To increase the chances of a song being a hit and get more airplay, how it sounds and its message has to be relevant to the audience and time. So many genres have evolved over the years and artists who didn't adapt to new sounds have

disappeared and are out of business; most got broke.

Below is a piece I wrote on the 8th of November 2018 and posted on my personal Facebook account, it's about making relevant music. It has a few tips and examples and I hope you can learn a thing or two.

Aspiring Artist Take Notes:

Other people in other countries don't eat chicken feet but we cook and braai them here in Mzansi. It's, therefore, RELEVANT to sell chicken feet in South Africa. Whatever you do as an artist, it's very important to consider RELEVANCY. Relevancy simply means doing the (1) right thing at a (2) right place, (3) right time, and (4) for or to the right people.

Relevancy means going with times and situations. Here is the best example of striving to be RELEVANT as an artist. Cassper Nyovest is doing his #FillUp Concert next month in KZN, Moses Mabhida Stadium. Today he dropped a song featuring the legendary KZN's very own Maskandi duo 'Shwi Nomtekhala' on KZN's biggest radio station 'Ukhozi FM.' You may find that the song with Shwi Nomtekhala was recorded years ago or just a few days before the event but he knew it would be more RELEVANT to drop it now that he's doing the concert in KZN...RELEVANCY.

Nyovest is also likely to put Shwi Nomtekhala on the #FillUpMosesMabhida lineup to attract the Maskandi fanatics most of which are based in KZN. Take a screenshot of this. Since KZN is the home of Maskandi, it's a million times relevant to put Maskandi acts on the line up to attract the masses.

@Touchline_Punchline, a rapper/lyricist from Thembisa dropped a rap video as a tribute to the late, legendary freedom fighter, Winnie Mandela soon as she passed away when the news was still trending and the late Akhumzi featured him on LIVE AMP for the tribute show of Mama Winnie Mandela. A few days ago Touchline performed on

SABC 1's Expressions, a song about women abuse because the song was RELEVANT to the topic discussed on the show the day.

But a huge MISTAKE that artists make when trying to be relevant is; they make songs based on TRENDS that don't have value and don't last and when those TRENDS die, those songs die also. It's wise to weigh

Colani "SooPurB"

the significance of a TREND before you leverage on it as an artist or any business. Make music about things that affect the country all the time, dark or blue people will be touched by your music. When your song or move is relevant to the people, they will pay attention because they relate. All the best in your hustle.

Yours Truly @SooPurBtheking

And guess what? Things happened as I predicted about Cassper Nyovest's KZN concert. Shwi Nomtekhala was part of the line-up. Before you sell something to people, it's wise to first check if they need it otherwise you might stock and sell meat to vegetarians and that's a total loss.

CHAPTER 2

Music Registration

Music is registered for two main reasons; to be rightfully protected and for royalties to be paid to the rightful owners when their music is

used or played on radio, TV programmes, movies, etc. If your song is not registered, somebody can steal it and make money from it. We've seen and heard of such cases a million times so for your copyright or ownership of your music as your intellectual property to be protected, you must register.

For your music to be protected and royalties paid by music users (radio, TV, stores, etc.) you must register with the following CMO's; (1) RISA, (2) SAMRO, (3) SAMPRA, and (4) CAPASSO. These are the main and major but not the only existing institutions in South Africa.

CMO stands for Collective Management Organisation. CMO's are non- profit organisations that license musical work to users, monitor usage, collect royalties, and disseminatethe royalties to the musicians and publishers who are their registered members.

These organisations are based in Gauteng but you can apply for memberships no matter where you are using their respective different remote membership application methods. I tried to outline the details of how one can go about applying for membership on each.

(1) RISA - Recording Industry of South Africa, is a trade association representing the collective interests of producers of music sound recordings of South Africa. RISA deals specifically with copyright. Copyright is the ownership that songwriters and composers have over every song they produce. It gives them protection from people copying, sharing, selling, and

recording the song without permission.

How do you apply for a RISA membership?

1. Go to the RISA website www.risa.org.za[1]
2. Click on 'Join RISA' to sign up on the portal, your name and contact details are required...a link to RESET YOUR PASSWORD will be sent to your email.
3. Open your email and click "RESET YOUR PASSWORD."
4. Once you've RESET YOUR PASSWORD you'll be able to log on to your portal to register by clicking "LOG ON/ REGISTER."
5. Click on "CREATE A NEW ARTIST." If you're a group you click the

same button.

1. You fill-in the required details thoroughly. If you're a group you add each member as "REPRESENTATIVE."

IF YOU COME ACROSS SOMETHING YOU'RE NOT SURE ABOUT, CALL RISA CONSULTANTS TO GET HELP...THEY ARE HIRED AND PAID TO HELP YOU.

Tel: (+27)118861342 and email: reception@risa.org.za

Once your RISA membership application is successful, you receive an ISRC for your songs and one for music videos. An ISRC code is made up of four parts; the country code, registrant code, year in which the song is commercially released, and designation code.

Country Code; this part of the code is made up of two letters that represent the country in which the applicant (artist or label) is based i.e. ZA represents South Africa. This part of the code is allocated by RISA from whom you obtain your ISRC code. Please note that no matter where in the world you release your music, you must always use

1. http://www.risa.org.za/

the country code you have been given because any changes to this part of the ISRC may result in duplicate codes.

The second part of the ISRC; Registrant Code. This section is made up of three alpha-numeric (letters and numbers) digits e.g 4RY which, when used with the allocated country code, is unique to you the applicant. This part of the code is issued by RISA in South Africa. As with the country code, you must not change this part of the code because it may result in duplication of codes and losing copyrights.

The third part; Year of Reference – this part of the code is made up of the last two digits of the year in which an ISRC code is assigned to a track i.e. 21 represents 2021 – the registrant is responsible for issuing this part of the code. If you release songs in 2022, you will change this part of the code to

22. If you release it in 2030 you change it to 30.

And the fourth part; Designation Code. This section is made up of five numeric digits i.e. 00001, 00002, etc. which are unique to each track in any given year. Once it's complete the ISRC code will look like ZA-4RY-21-00001 (for the first track released in 2021).

Please note that you will not need the hyphens (-) when embedding (attaching) the codes into your songs. These are used in the written format to enable codes to be read and checked easily. Different computer and cellphone apps are used to embed ISRC codes to songs, Google will help you with that. The software programs also allow you to add other song details such as the artist cover and metadata.

(2) SAMRO - South African Music Rights Organisation. It is the primary representative of music Performing Rights in Southern Africa. SAMRO's role is the administration of music, distribution of royalties, and promotes copyright law of composers and authors' works, through the collection of license fees from television broadcasters, radio stations, in-store radio stations, pubs, clubs, retailers, restaurants, and all other businesses that broadcast music.

To apply for a SAMRO membership, follow the steps below:

Step 1: Go to the SAMRO website www.samro.org.za[2] and click on 'CREATOR APPLICATION.'

2. http://www.samro.org.za/

Step 2: Download the FORMS required (1) Membership application form; requires your details (2) Deed of Assignments form; giving SAMRO a go- ahead to administer your performance rights and collect royalties on your behalf (3) Notification of Works form; requires information about the songs you claim ownership of. (4) Banking Details Update form; requires your banking details to which SAMRO will pay your royalties. You can

download the forms one by one or all at once.

Step 3: You must fill in and send back to SAMRO all 4 forms accordingly and put your initials on every page. If there is something you're struggling with, contact SAMRO via telephone or email for clarification.

Scan the forms (use your phone, download any scanning app you can get on Play Store or iStore). Send the forms together with a certified copy of your ID and Proof of Residence to the customer services email address, fax number, or hand-deliver them to their offices during working hours. You can contact SAMRO after 4 weeks to check the progress of your application.

SAMRO contact details; Tel: +27 11712 8000 and email: customerservices@ samro.org.za and the best advice I can give you is that you must always call to follow-up otherwise you might wait forever.

Once you are a member and have received your membership or relation number, SAMRO will give you access to your SAMRO online portal. You will then type "SAMRO portal" on Google or any search engine of your choice and use your relation number as both your username and your password to access your portal.

In your portal, you will be able to access all data, register all your new songs and check payments (previous and pending). You will not get paid for a song if you have NOT registered/notified it.

You need to register your songs and your splits correctly. Make sure you have agreed on the songwriting splits (%) with anyone you worked with on each song before you register the song with SAMRO. If I produced a song, and someone else sang on it, I normally just go 50/50 with that person.

Make sure you have agreed on the shares and put them in writing. If you notify a song and your split or share doesn't match the ones of the other people involved in the song, SAMRO won't pay out your royalties until the splits correlate because each person has to notify the song individually and the as the same as others

Your SAMRO portal allows you to register your new songs quite easily and efficiently. Simply click "MY MUSIC" on the left-hand panel, then "New Notification". If you were involved in the composition of the song your role is "Composer" and if you wrote lyrics, your role will be "Author."

(3) SAMPRA - South African Music Performance Rights Association. SAMPRA's basic mission is to give music licenses to businesses that use music such as shops, restaurants, clubs, etc., and "needletime royalties" which are then paid to music owners (artists and record labels). A relevant unfortunate example is that of Woolworths having decided NOT to renew their SAMPRA license; Woolworths stores will no longer play South African music, which means an income stream for Mzansi music creators has been shut down. Now as artists we pray that other stores that play our music and pay royalties DO NOT follow Woolworths because if they do, our livelihoods will be negatively impacted.

It is FREE of charge to apply for a SAMPRA membership for both artists and record companies. You can apply on the #SAMPRAApp which you can download on Google Play Store if you're using an Android device or Apple iStore if you have iPhone. Alternatively, you can apply via their website.

Step 1: Go to the SAMPRA website www.sampra.org.za[3] and click on 'APPLY FOR MEMBERSHIP.'

Step 2: Since downloading and printing the forms is a long process, just

choose online forms and apply right away.

Once your application is successful and you or your record company can then notify/register your music online via the website or the app. It is that easy, simple, and quick.

The SAMPRA app also allows you to send emails, chat, and enquire about anything instantly. For more information call SAMPRA on 011 5619 660 or contact them via email: info@sampra.org.za

(4) CAPASSO - a mechanical rights licensing organisation based in Johannesburg, South Africa, it collects and distributes mechanical

3. http://www.sampra.org.za/

royalties to its members; composers (producers and artists) and publisher (record labels & other publishing companies). 'Mechanical' rights are the right to reproduce a piece of music onto CDs, DVDs, records, or tapes. Mechanical royalties are generated when a song or music is sold either via CDs or online and CAPASSO represents artists and music owners in that regard.

To apply for a CAPASSO membership you follow the steps outlined below:

1. Visit www.capasso.co.za [4]and open the membership tap.
2. Click on the 'Type' of registration you require; (i) Composer (Individual)

or (ii) Publisher (Company).

1. Fill-in the application and attach; 1.Your certified ID Copy, 2. Bank Confirmation Letter and 3. Proof of Payment (R100 Membership Fee) must be paid, bank details available on the website.

For more and specific inquiries contact CAPASSO consultants on the

Tel: following;

Membership Query membership@capasso.co.za

Notifications Query Notifications@capasso.co.za

Also, get hold of CAPASSO on social media. Twitter: @CAPASSOHub and Facebook: @CAPASSOHub.

For each of the above organisations to serve you as an artist, producer, or record label, you need to be a member. And for each of them to be able to monitor your music usage (airplay) and sales, you need to notify them of each song you release. If your song is not on their systems, they won't be able to monitor its usage and as a result, you won't get the royalties due to you.

We've also heard cases whereby artists have notified their songs correctly and on time but the payments and reports don't match the actual airplay and sales records provided by these CMO's. So it is wise

4. http://www.capasso.co.za/

and significant for music creators, publishers, and record labels to have other airplay monitoring options in place.

There is a company called "Radio Monitor" to which you can subscribe or sign up to get comprehensive and accurate data/information showing you which stations (radio and TV) are playing your songs (audio and visuals) and how many plays/spins your song is getting.

Radio Monitor is a global company, Jarrod Aston-Assenheim is the person in charge of Radio Monitor in South Africa. You can send him an email to enquire and sign up jarrod@radiomonitor.co.za and the last I checked, the start-up cost was R750 once-off.

You add ALL the songs you've already released on your initial account registration (if you've had your stuff play on radio and TV, it's worth it). Any future releases are charged at R550 per song. Check out their website www.radiomonitor.co.za [5]for more specific information.

5. http://www.radiomonitor.co.za/

CHAPTER 3

Music Publishing

Music publishing is the administration of (1) getting your music or a song registered with the various CMOs I discussed in the previous chapter, (2) issuing licenses to people and establishments that want to use the music, (3) monitoring broadcasts and performances (airplay), collecting royalties from the music users (radio, TV, supermarkets, etc.) and distributing royalties to respective copyright owners. If you're not registered with these organisations no matter how high your songs can be rotated or played you won't get a cent.

A publishing deal is when an artist gives certain percentages of copyright/ ownership of their music to a publisher or publishing company in exchange for publishing services. An example would be a publishing company taking 30% profit from a song by SooPurB and in return provide him with their services. Publishers also play the role of pitching the music of their clients/ partners to television programmes, ads, video games, movies, etc. to make more money for themselves and their clients.

When royalties are paid through CMO's the publisher will take a certain as per the agreement or contract between the company and the artist. Percentages vary with companies and agreements, some deals can be 50/50 depending on various factors.

Royalties are money paid to the owners of the song and are split or shared among everyone involved in the making of the composition according to the amount of stake or percent each party is set to get.

Two or more artists working on one song can have different publishing companies. Each company will monitor the percentage of its artist and take the amount or share of royalties they agreed upon. There are different types of royalties namely performance royalties, mechanical royalties, needle time royalties, and synchronisation royalties.

Performance royalties are paid to songwriters (for writing lyrics), composers (creating melodies), and publishers when a particular song performed or played in public. These are the royalties generated when a song is played in supermarkets, restaurants, a doctor's waiting room, gym, etc. These establishments need to obtain licenses from the music owners and they pay royalties in a form of license fees.

A sub-category of performance royalties is needletime royalties. Needletime royalties are collected by SAMPRA and paid to its members; recording artists, background singers, instrumentalists (drummers, guitarists, saxophonists, etc.), and everyone who contributed to the making of a song. The importance of needletime royalties is that they cater to musicians who did not write and compose a recording but did play other roles as mentioned above.

And another vital thing to know about needle time is that it doesn't replace or get deducted from other royalty streams. It is paid by the music users or broadcasters as an extra fee to the other licensing fees or types of royalties.

Mechanical royalties are paid to the record owners whenever a copy of their music is made. Mechanical royalties are generated when a song or music is printed on CDs, downloaded online, used as a ringtone (and/or caller tune or welcome tone), or streamed/played on online interactive platforms such as Spotify, Deezer, iTunes, etc.

Interactive streaming platforms are the ones that allow the user to choose the music they listen to. Non-Interactive platforms do not allow users to choose what to listen to e.g. radio and TV stations and they pay performance royalties instead of mechanical royalties.

The difference between mechanical and performance royalties is that mechanical royalties are royalties generated when the music sells through hard copies and online platforms, and performance royalties are generated when the music is played in public businesses and by broadcasters. And mechanical rights are administered by CAPASSO, performance rights are handled by SAMRO and SAMPRA handles the sub-category of performance rights, needle time rights.

Synchronisation or sync royalties are those that music owners earn when their song is used on visual content such as movies, video games, TV advertisements, TV shows, YouTube, etc. Before one can use someone's music on their visual content, he or she must first obtain a synchronisation license from the copyright owner(s). And if the visual piece is to be broadcast on public platforms such as TV, the copyright owners also generate performance royalties on top of the licensing fee.

The price of mechanical and performance royalties is determined by law in each country but synchronisation royalties are negotiated (in the process of requesting and obtaining a sync license) by the music owner(s) and the person who wants to use the music.

A sync license fee can be influenced by factors such as how much of the song will be used (whole or part of it), type of use (background music, commercial, movie trailer, etc.), original or cover, and territory (where the video will be displayed) either local, national or global.

CHAPTER 4

DISTRIBUTION

Distribution is the commercial activity of transporting and selling goods (i.e. music) from a producer (i.e. artist) to the consumers. Once your song, album, EP, or mixtape is readily packaged, the next thing to do is to distribute it to the people. Back in the days, most artists were selling cassettes and CD copies in the streets, carrying them on the boots of their cars and some still do it today. Artists who only wanted to promote their music would give copies to people and taxi drivers for free. Whether it is for money or free, it is still music distribution.

Artists in the past also relied on music stores that were selling physical copies of cassettes and CDs. This method required artists, managers, and record companies to identify distribution companies that worked directly with these stores. Artists and record labels would enter into contractual agreements with the distributors. The contracts were mainly about the percentages of profits each party would take per copy sold. Distributors would mostly agree to work with artists and labels whose music was in- demand or had the potential to sell.

However, things have evolved and technology is advancing daily. Cassettes are no longer sold hence cassette players also are now extinct but this method of distribution still exists, as a result, we still see and purchase physical CD copies on shelves though they're also almost old news. The birth of online and digital music stores has immensely shifted and radically revolutionised the music distribution business.

Now there are companies known as DSPs (Digital Service Providers) that offer online distribution deals and services. You can have your music distributed and sold online by companies such as The Orchard (home to the songbird, Berita, Saudi, and more South African artists and indie labels), Africori (home to Sho Madjozi, Master KG, and most of the new wave Hip Hop artists), Content Connect Africa (home to Holly Rey, SooPurB, and more other South African musicians and record companies). These companies agree with artists on profit splits depending on various factors.

Also, some companies distribute an artist's music as long as it meets their requirements. We have companies such as DITTO, CD Run, CD Baby (used by A-reece) DistroKid, TuneCore (used by Touchline), and more others. Some of these companies require an annual fee e.g. as I write this book, DITTO costs R200 to host one artist per year and you can upload as many songs as you want.

These digital distributors have numerous packages for independent artists and record labels. There are also packages to get your song featured on various local and global playlists which artists can also pay for to increase the numbers of streams and profits.

Artists can now sell their music online from their mobile devices. Recently, I uploaded a couple of songs for artists using my cellphone. On DSPs, the performances of songs are reported directly to you via e-mail, you can also check anytime you want and payments are also done digitally straight to your bank account.

The best thing to do is to check the terms and conditions of each company more especially its reach and profit-sharing percentages, and then choose one that you think is best for you, your music and your brand. You don't need a record label to do this, you can do it independently and no middleman will cut your already cut profits.

However, as an emerging artist whose music is not yet in-demand, you better look for ways to get your music heard free of charge. In South Africa, for instance, the majority of music consumers download music for free from websites such as Fakaza.com. Dj Maphorisa and Kabza De Small have been using Fakaza to get their amapiano albums to the masses and as a result, having their songs played everywhere in the country the same day of release.

The two DJs are big enough to put their music on online stores and get large numbers of people buying and streaming but it seems like their aim has been just to get the music everywhere and fast and when their songs flood the streets, they get booked left, right and centre. Although Maphorisa and

Kabza put out music for free, it's surprising that their songs also dominate and sell more online. So it seems like popularity also boosts online sales. Seemingly giving out music for free has subtly yet extravagantly boosted their sales and streaming numbers.

Even big South African artists who only put their music online to be purchased and streamed are admitting that their music gets to the masses mostly through these free blogs. These blogs buy the music from the online stores and put it out for free downloads. As much as these free music downloading sites don't financially benefit artists, they play a huge role in getting the music to clubs, cars, and every corner quickly.

So my advice to emerging artists is that one needs to consider distributing music using both online stores, streaming platforms, and sites that allow free downloading. While the minority with access to online stores and streaming platforms buy and stream your music, the majority that downloads for free get you popularised hence you get bookings - paid for gigs.

CHAPTER 5

PR (PUBLIC RELATIONS)

PR is the cornerstone of any brand, whether an individual or corporate brand. It's not only how people get to know about a brand but also how to sell that brand and get people to believe in it. It's a very hard job. - Molife Kumona

PR is the practice of strategically managing the spread of music and news of (and about) a musician to the public through different media platforms such as radio, television, newspapers, blogs, social media, etc. It is mainly about getting an artist and their music exposed to the public through the mediums.

Another significant role of PR is to make sure that an artist's image, name, and reputation are always clean in the public eye more especially when the artist is involved in bad acts and scandals. A PR must ensure that the public perception about the artist remains positive otherwise the artist's career might be badly affected or unfortunately come to an end.

In the music business, the basic role of PR companies or strategists is to make sure that songs by artists are playing on radio stations, music videos are playing on TV, artists get interviews on radio, appear and perform on TV, featured in newspapers and other platforms. A PR's job is to gun for exposure for the music and the musician by putting or plugging them on various platforms. It is the job of a PR to call radio stations and convince music compilers that a song is worthy to be played and most importantly repeated.

PR companies and PR managers are very expensive to hire. Just sampling or plugging one song on radio without getting interviews, can cost around R20 000 or even more, it depends on various factors such as seasons and negotiations. The lowest PR you can get to just to plug your song on radio

Colani "SooPurB"

can be R5000 but it's also rare and chances are that they're still new and trying to establish themselves. However, you can do it yourself if you invest your time and energy to study and practice it.

"How do you get into magazines? How can you get on TV or in your local newspaper? What can you do so others will take notice of your art? When I was first trying to get noticed, all of these questions went through my mind. After a lot of trial and error and a lot of reading, I began to understand the world of public relations." - Mark Edward

Big PR companies charge monthly e.g. 20k per month for 3 months and that's straight-up 60k. In the first month, they can maybe sample or send out the song, making follow-ups in the second month, and then get you interviews in the third month. And an artist can pay fully for all three months, get their song play-listed radio, and do interviews, TV appearances, performances, newspaper features, and all, only to find that the song does not blow up. So paying PR doesn't guarantee success it's just a business risk.

I always tell my fellow artists that releasing a song is more like gambling - playing lotto. You spend money hoping to win but if it's not your time it's not time, all you got to do is play again; release a new song, and promote it. If you're an artist that is broke and obviously can't afford PR like myself it doesn't mean it's the end of the road. I did get my songs played on a couple of radio stations, appeared and performed on eTV - Shiz Live, SABC 1 - YoTV Live, and featured on national newspapers without hiring a PR.

Like I said in the 'About the Author' part of this book that being an intern producer at SABC (Ligwalagwala FM) helped me learn first-hand the professional processes, requirements, and ways of getting one's song play- listed on radio stations and requesting interviews. However, the very same information is available on the internet, books, and most radio stations have put up the very same information on their websites for anyone to freely access.

Once your song is complete and you've registered (or notified) it on your CMO's, the next thing you need to professionally and thoroughly prepare is your PRESS KIT. A Press Kit, also known as a 'Media Kit' is a pre-packaged set of promotional material that provides information about you as an artist or band. Boxes that you need to tick to have a full press kit as an artist are,

(1) Biography (Bio/Profile), (2) Press Release, and (3) Press Photos. These 3 are needed in newspapers but when you send your song to radio you also need to add (4) the song and (5) Art Cover (Artwork).

Colani "SooPurB"

Below is an example of a press release. You write it as a separate document and if you like you can include the song details on it instead of the email body.

PRESS RELEASE

FOR IMMEDIATE RELEASE: 8 JANUARY 2021

SooPurB drops a single titled "Ngigcwele".

Siswati Hip Hop sensation, SooPurB drops his new and latest musical

offering; a single titled Ngigcwele.

On his birthday last year, 16 April 2020, SooPurB released his first-ever body of work; a four-track EP titled KWASUKASUKELA. Now he kickstarts 2021 with this hot Amapiano flavoured Hip Hop track aiming to rock all the four seasons of the year.

This new single is proof that SooPurB is indeed one of the few talents to look out for this year and it also solidifies his versatility and writing skills. As a proudly Siswati speaker, he flows effortlessly with his mother tongue with a fusion of English.

NGIGCWELE is a song with which SooPurB shamelessly expresses his feelings of love to the goddess that gives him goosebumps. Unlike most intimate relationships that exist nowadays whereby people don't communicate their intentions about the person, they claim to love, in this song SooPurB frankly mentions his plans about him and the lady he is attracted to.

On this project, SooPurB has worked with his homeboy Bheki "Jay Beats"

Malaza.

Radio stations accept songs in different ways. Some stations want the song as an mp3 file, some want a link to a wav file and some require you to upload your song on their websites. So it is a must to check how each radio station you submit your music to accepts songs. First impressions are important at all times so your press kit has to be professionally packaged. Don't send photos of you eating at a restaurant captured using your cellphone; do a professional photo shoot and have the photos superbly edited. Also, get a proper writer and designer to do your profile and artworks. Of course, you need to pay up to get all these things done.

Colani "SooPurB"

When you send your song to radio, the following details MUST accompany your press kit. I'll use my details to show you how it's done. With the blue words, I'm trying to explain further so don't include that in your email.

SUBJECT LINE: MUSIC SUBMISSION

Greetings,

Kindly find the song submission for Siswati rapper from Mpumalanga, SOOPURB.

Song Details:

1. Artist/Group Name: SOOPURB
2. Song Title: SKELEM
3. Genre: HIP HOP
4. Language: SISWATI/ENGLISH
5. Author: COLANI "SOOPURB" NKOSI

(An author is a songwriter, full names and surname as per your ID are required and if you featured someone you'll add their full names as well).

1. Composer: MANDLA "DJ SHOLLY" SHONGWE (A composer is a beatmaker, Dj Sholly is his stage name).
2. Publisher: e.g. SOOPURB PUBLISHING

(If you don't have one you can write SAMRO and that's if you're a SAMRO member, if you're not, then register first).

1. Record Label/Company: SOOPURB ENTERTAINMENT. (If you don't have you can write NONE or INDEPENDENT).

19. ISRC: ZA-5RY-20-00001.

(You get this code if you're a RISA member if you're not, go register). Remember each song must have its own ISRC, the ZA and the 5RY remain the same so you only change 20, which is the year in which you're releasing and the track number. For track 2 it'll be like ZA-5RY-00002).

Colani "SooPurB"

Attachments: Mp3 file, Art Cover, Press Release & Artist's Bio/ Profile

Looking forward to hearing from you soon.

Regards,

Colani Nkosi

Contact: 0720138921

(You'll then attach your song as a file or link depending on the station's requirement, attach your bio/profile, press release, song artwork & press photos. If your photos are stored online either on Dropbox, Google Drive, or similar storages you can just provide a link. You can send a song to radio without including press photos but should they need to interview you they'll need your photos to do a social media poster, so having them ready is important).

A complete and professional email to radio stations will look like this: SUBJECT; MUSIC SUBMISSION

Greetings

I hope this email finds you well. Kindly find the song submission for Mpumalanga's very own talented singer, songwriter, and record producer, SooPurB.

Label Copy:-

Title: NGIGCWELE

Artist: SOOPURB

Genre: HIP HOP (SISWATI & ENGLISH)

Duration: 03:58

Author/Composers: COLANI NKOSINATHI NKOSI Publisher: SELF-RELEASE/INDEPENDENT

ISRC: ZA-4RY-21-00001

Samro: 2292938

Attachments: Mp3 file, Bio & Press Release.

Looking forward to hearing from you.

Colani "SooPurB"

Regards Colani Nkosi 0720138921

You don't necessarily have to copy and paste my email as it is but make sure you keep it sweet and short. By looking at your subject line, the compiler or music receiver must know that it's a song being submitted and the song details should be provided fully as I did.

After sending your song through, it is best to call the compiler to check if they have received it because emails act funny at times. And calling in might make them not forget to listen to your song because they receive a lot. Also, when you call, kindly ask of the possible day they'll possibly listen to your song and ask when next you should call to check if the song is approved or not. If they give you a date write it down and call again on that date or the day after.

If you do not have a compiler's office number just call the station's reception; they will connect you to him or her. If you also do not have the station's reception number look for it on their social media pages or website. Hell yeah, it costs plenty of airtime to call office numbers but that's what you have to invest in if you want to get your song played.

Lately network service providers have different prices of minutes to call any network which is a bit cheaper than just using airtime so take advantage of such services if you have to call office telephone numbers.

Another important thing you got to know about sampling or sending music to radio stations is the fact that different stations play different types of music. You can't send a Hip Hop nor a house music song to a Christianity radio station. Each radio has its audience, pace, taste, and sound.

Some commercial radio stations in South Africa do not play music by unknown artists. So do not waste energy and resources sending music to irrelevant stations. Do your homework and know the types of radio stations that are likely to play your shit and send your song to them.

Listening to a radio station and knowing the different shows and their features is what you need to do if you want to win at sampling your music to relevant recipients. You can't succeed at any business that you know nothing about so get informed as possible as you can.

Once you get confirmation that your song is included on a station's playlist, the next thing to do is to request an interview. An interview request is sent to either a programmes manager or content producer of a show. Well, if you know the shows of a station, you'll also know the show that is likely to host you depending on the style of music you do. Programmes managers or show producers' emails and contact details can be obtained from their receptionist.

If you're lucky to have all the e-mails, the programmes manager's, show producer's and the compiler's, it's wise to include them all in the email because the programmes manager is the one authorising your request, the producer is the one scheduling your interview and the compiler schedules your song according to the time agreed upon by all parties. However, they cc each other. Compared to other media platforms such as newspapers, television, online blogs and others, radio is the most difficult one to penetrate because of its nature and processes, departments and people involved. On a newspaper, if the journalist is happy about your press kit they write the story and submit to the editor and you get featured.

On the 12th of November 2018 I wrote and posted a piece on Facebook about focusing and using your energy to send your music (always with your press/media kit along) to media platforms that will give you maximum exposure for free rather than spamming individuals on social media who will not bother entertaining your shit because you're still unknown. Here is the piece, I hope you'll learn something from it.

Aspiring Artist Take Notes:

Ever since I appeared and performed on eTV (Shiz Live), a lot of aspiring rappers have been flooding my inbox asking how I made it happen. Well, I never had a problem with that, I SHARE with them the exact method I used to impress the Shiz Live producer. I secretly follow each of those who asked me and I'm amazed because NONE OF THEM is making any move.

Okay, I don't give a damn whether they try or not, I told them what they wanted to know and I can't push them to act. Well, with this post I wanna focus on the artists that, after my TV appearance, have been asking me to listen to their music. I wish one of them can give me a straightforward reason why he or she wanted me to listen and tell me what it is that they expected to do after. Sadly, I couldn't listen to anyone's music due to lack of DATA but even if I did, I HONESTLY WAS GONA DO NOTHING.

I get a chance to listen to good music at times but as an artist that is also struggling, I do nothing besides complementing. My advice to fellow upcoming artists; instead of wasting time, energy and data sending music to other artists, use those little resources to send your music to ONLINE BLOGS, MEDIA OUTLETS (RADIO, TV, PAPERS) etc. BUT FIRSTLY LEARN THE RIGHT WAYS TO SUBMIT TO EACH.

Send your music where you might be given a platform to showcase your talent to the masses. Major artists steal songs of upcoming artists and use them for their benefit. Sort out your music registrations to get your shit protected. Stop sending your music to artists, send it to the masses through the media.

Yours Truly @SooPurBtheking

On one of the pieces I wrote on the 6th of November 2018 and posted on Facebook, I spoke about the power of radio. Well, I'm not saying other media platforms are less important, I just wanted to outline how radio was used by Hitler to spread his ideologies and as a result, millions of Jews got killed. Also, radio is one platform that pays royalties to artists. Music continues to generate money even after the creators have passed away and that's bread and butter to their children and families.

Aspiring Artist Take Notes:

Adolf Hitler killed millions of Jews in Germany during his tenure. He did not kill these millions on his own but he managed to spread and inject into the majority of native German people's minds his ideology of getting rid of all Jews. Question is: HOW DID HITLER SPREAD OUT HIS MESSAGES THAT GOT MILLIONS OF JEWS

TORTURED AND BRUTALLY MURDERED BY GERMANS? The answer is RADIO. The lunatic used radio.

He did not go to the studio to broadcast but he made sure that the radio presenters and producers preach his ideology of killing all Jews. Check history to find out why he wanted them all killed, I'm just gonna focus on the power of this thing called RADIO. Even today radio is still one of the few powerful mediums artists depend on.

Where did Boity drop her first single? On Metro FM's Fresh Breakfast and it trended for days. A lot of big South African acts drop their songs on Metro FM these days. Though they drop songs on Metro FM they make sure their songs are plugged in all radio stations in the country. Unlike TV, radio is mobile, it's in cars, phones, shops etc. People listen to radio while driving, washing, cooking, shopping, and security guards while on duty. But TV needs you to put your ass on a sofa and keep your eyes on it.

Make sure radio is on your PR plan for your next project. Last year I wasn't gonna get my song Nkebelele to 1k downloads in 17 days if it wasn't for radio. Before dropping the song I dropped hot rap verses live on radio (Ligwalagwala FM's Hip Hop show) every Friday in July 2017.

Yours Truly

@SooPurBtheking

Another platform that you can also use to expose your brand and music to the masses is print media. Newspapers and magazines, unlike radio, they allow the public or readers to see you because a feature article is accompanied by your photo(s). And the people also get to see exactly how your artistic name is spelt. For example, my artistic name is SooPurB and through radio, listeners only hear the pronunciation which is that of "superb" but on a newspaper people see the spelling as it is.

Of course, each media platform has its PR benefits, all platforms combined serve a greater purpose and help you obtain a wider reach and exposure. A person can hear your song and name on radio but they ain't seeing you. On the other hand, in print media, a reader can see your face and see how your name is spelt but they ain't hearing your song. And TV affords viewers a chance to hear the song and see the artist's performance. So each platform is important in its unique way.

However, nowadays we're technologically advanced so we can go live via social media networks while doing a radio interview. We also have online platforms such as websites, blogs, YouTube and others that allow anybody to listen to music and read the news at any time and they can do it repeatedly because they are in full control of such platforms unlike on radio and TV, if you miss a song or interview, you cannot rewind.

For an artist's song and brand to gain maximum exposure, it's significant to penetrate all the platforms at their disposal. A press kit is all that is needed from an artist to be easily featured on each platform. Let me be honest with you, not anyone can create the best media kit for you and if your media kit sucks, your chances of being rejected are just high. So pay a skilled photographer, a skilled designer and a skilled writer. Check people's track records before trusting them with your brand.

No matter which platform you aspire to be featured on, all you got to do is to get their contact details (email and contact number), send your request accompanied by your press kit and then call them up to check if your stuff is in order. Your dream won't come true if you don't put in the work. No one was born knowing how to do all these things and most of the people who are excelling didn't even go to school, they're self-taught specialists.

"It's not a 9 to 5 job. You do PR everywhere you go". - Lauren Robinson

I watched one of the Slikour On Life -YouTube shows, "Speedsta In The Park" and he hosted two ladies (Sivu Mfenyana and Lwazi Zondo) who are PR specialists at Sony Music (ZA). One of the PR specialists, Sivu studied law but she practices PR. So all it takes is putting in work, do the mistakes, learn and kick ass. Staying at home waiting for a record label to discover you is a lost course, the clock is ticking so move.

Since the beginning of this chapter I talk about different media people in different positions such as journalists, editors, music compilers, content producers, programmes managers and more, therefore, you have to learn how to work with people, be nice and professional otherwise no one will want to help or work with you at all. You need to be careful when you make requests and making follow-ups and not be a nuisance.

Since you're the one who needs help from these media people, you must be patient with them because they're dealing with thousands of people who are sending music and requesting interviews as you do. Don't give them a reason to choose others and put you aside. Also, understand that they prioritise famous artists because they are of public interest.

Keep in mind that the South African entertainment industry is too small, most people know each other and as they meet at events they share the news. Messing with one person might close lots of doors for you. So you have to friendly and maintain good relationships with the media people because your career depends on them. The media will forever be powerful and capable of creating superstars and also destroying them.

Also, the way you treat people in general, other artists and supporters, has a major impact on your reputation. How the people see you and talk about you, are things to take into consideration no matter what you do. That one person you're rude to either on DMs, comments or wherever, he or she will tell others about their encounter with you, one person tells the next and that's how bad news quickly spread about you.

> *"It is far less impactful what you say about yourself, compared to what others say about you." - Pap Boachie-Yiadom*

No matter how famous you become, the way you treat and work with people will determine your longevity in the game. Even how you live your personal life has an impact on your career and the media will always hunt you to spread the good and the bad you do. At times it's not what you do that affects you and your career but anything you're involved in or linked with. It's key to mind what and who you associate yourself with.

An example of how bad news negatively affect an artist's career is that of South Africa's well-known musician, Sjava, he got removed from events he was set to perform at and also taken off award nominations after his ex- girlfriend, Lady Zamar had alleged that he abused her and opened a rape case against him.

When this happened, Sjava wasn't even charged yet but the bad news was already and heavily affecting his career and livelihood. Him getting cancelled from shows, it meant losing income. Although Sjava was still awaiting trial, many people were already perceiving him as a rapist. Public perception is the heart, soul and life of an artist's career.

So an artist needs to try and avoid being linked with scandals and any form of bad news because they destroy one's hard-earned success.

Another example would be that of Mampintsha assaulting his girlfriend, Babes Wodumo. The public was even demanding that his music gets cut off from radio and TV and promoters to stop booking him. Without airplay and bookings, an artist's career is as good as dead. Being mindful of your conduct both in public and in private is essential.

As much as PR helps get music exposed to the public, it also helps create a positive image for the musician. Minor incidents that artists might get involved in are easily mitigated through well planned and properly communicated PR messages but big issues and scandals such as rape and abuse are difficult to dodge and they kill careers of artists.

Worldwide known RnB superstar, R-Kelly ended behind bars for sexual assault cases. South African Kwaito star, Brickz also ended in jail because of rape. These artists have worked so hard to become household names but being accused and found guilty of rape has tarnished the fame and annihilated the legacies it took them years to build.

Another well-known South African artist that suffered and fortunately survived negative publicity is none other than Mpumalanga's very own, Ntokozo "K.O" Mdluli. When Cashtime, a record company and clothing label he co-owned took off, he dropped a smash hit "Caracara" featuring KidX, who was one of the artists that were part of the gang. The song impacted the South African Hip Hop culture hugely and positively and K.O defiantly broke boundaries and became a game-changer with the Skanda sound.

A year later tables turned upside-down when things weren't going well for the other artists in the label. Ma-e, Maggz, Nomoozlie and KidX, all didn't shine as the public anticipated and K.O was accused of holding them back. The album that K.O dropped after the label's failure didn't do well. It took him great efforts to restore his reputation and getting the public to support him again.

As much as bad publicity resulting from scandals, bad associations and bad conduct can destroy one's career, good publicity resulting from good behaviour, and good reputation attracts great opportunities. Artists such as Caspper Nyovest, Aka, Kwesta and others are getting millions from deals simply because their names are not linked with dirt, bad behaviour and negativity.

Cassper Nyovest has been getting deals after deals because he keeps his brand clean. He got deals from major brands such as MTN, Ciroc, Samsung and more. Aka got Cruz Vodka, Reebok among others. Kwesta also got to collaborate with brands like Telkom, Jameson and Heineken which got him to do songs with American rappers, Rich Homie Quan and Rick Ross.

K.O's Skhanda World merchandise ended up being sold at Studio 88 stores across the country and he also got an ASICS sneakers deal. All these artists wouldn't be getting such deals if they were linked with rape, abuse and other forms of bad publicity. Big brands work with and spend millions on reputable artists.

"If I was down to the last dollar of my marketing budget I'd spend it on PR!" - Bill Gates

CHAPTER 6

HOW I MANAGED TO BE FEATURED ON PLATFORMS (RADIO, TV, PAPERS AND BLOGS)

On the previous chapter, I already talked about sending music to radio stations and requesting interviews. In this chapter, I just want to share

how I got featured on other platforms. I'll simply tell you how I got featured on eTV (Shiz Live), SABC (YoTV Live), Daily Sun, Mpumalanga News, Times of Swaziland and other platforms. I hope you'll learn from my tactics.

After seeing plenty of talented creatives making waves on social media and ending up getting featured on bigger platforms and becoming successful, I thought I should also try. Artists such as Mlindo The Vocalist, Indlovukazi and more others were noticed on social media by big artists who then assisted them to kick-start their careers.

Mlindo the Vocalist was posting on social media video clips of him and his brother singing and got noticed by Dj Maphorisa and the rest is history. Indlovukazi posted a video clip of herself singing on social media with a caption that she wishes to work with Black Coffee and Coffee asked Heavy K to work with her and the rest history. She then worked with Prince Kaybee and they together made one of the biggest songs of 2019. Many creatives used social media to their advantage and are now living their dreams.

On the second half of 2018, I started recording video clips of myself rapping to random beats of well-known songs and I posted on all my social media pages. I would tag the eTV Shiz Live producer on Twitter and she was impressed by my Siswati rap. She then asked for my contact number via DMs and she invited me to their Shiz Booth cypher recording in July.

I got to Red pepper studios on the 6th of July 2018 and did my thing and she told me to send her my music hinting chances of featuring me on the live show. I was already having her e-mail and contact number but since I had no new music I told myself that I'd send her my future releases. I watched Shiz Live the entire winter hoping they'll air my cypher clip but they UNFORTUNATELY didn't.

In September, she hit me up with a phone call and invited me for a live performance and interview and asked that I rock Siswati traditional attire because you know September is heritage month in Mzansi. Regardless of my trip being horrible I made it to the show and made my first TV appearance. It all happened as a result of posting clips on social media and tagging the right person. Yeah, that's how I got featured on eTV.

How did I know the producer? The answer is simple, I watched the show and they always show the names of the producers and those of the entire crew (both on-screen and behind the scenes). Although such information is normally shown at the end of the shows and the words are moving but you ain't gonna miss it if you watch a couple of times. You just get the name of the producer and then search him or her on social media (linked in is the best). If you find them, hit their DMs and don't text "Hi," "HUD," and all the other improper chatting language nonsense. Just greet, say who you are, what you need and why, all in one message.

Before you hit producers up, your press kit and music must be ready otherwise you're wasting their time and yours and they might not reply to you ever again. If you contact a producer of a show, your press kit and your music are the main things they ask. When the Shiz Live producer called me, she asked me to send through my bio and my song and I did right away because I had them ready. When I got to the studio, presenters didn't have to ask me who I am, where I come from, which tribe I represent and all, they had already learned everything about me from my bio.

Oh yeah, that's just how I got featured on eTV, I posted my video clips on social media and I got noticed. I knew the producer by getting her name from the moving words at the end of the show. I searched her on Twitter and started tagging her on my content. Blaq Diamond has signed Sbahle under their record label, Umuthi records. They discovered her on Instagram. She's been recording and posting videos of herself singing and the rest is history.

In 2019 I appeared and performed live on SABC 1's YoTV. Unlike of Shiz Live, here I didn't know the producer or anybody at Urban Brew (the company producing YoTV). I was put on by one of South Africa's best PR gurus, Lebo Mlangeni. Lebo also is CEO of Abuti PR, hence his nickname is Abuti and he's also the managing director of Jozi Entertainment.

Lebo and I have been friends on Facebook for a while and in February 2019. He posted on Facebook a behind the scenes photo of Ntando at YoTV on and I commented that I wish to be on the show and he told me to text him on WhatsApp. He asked me to send him my song and bio and in a few minutes he replied to give me a date and we negotiated the price. That's how I got to YoTV.

I've already spoken about how expensive PR services can be but if you can afford one just go for it because you won't be worried about getting your songs on radio, interviews, TV appearances and your brand on papers and other platforms.

Before Lebo plugged me on YoTV, I already had the producer's email address as they showed it on-screen during the show. I was already on a mission to send my song and media kit with the hope that I'd be invited to the show but the "Law of Attraction" worked its wonders and brought Lebo "Abuti PR" Mlangeni to help before I could even take a step.

Many artists hit me up on social media asking that I share with them the secret strategy I used to get on TV. I always assure them that there's no secret at all. There's no magic needed to be featured on a platform, either TV, radio, newspaper etc. Artists believe it's a secret because they do not contact these platforms to make enquiries. Just get your press kit ready, contact the platform you wanna be featured on.

Moving right along, let me share with you the tactics I used to be featured on newspapers and online entertainment websites and my experiences with each. Whenever I laid my hands on a newspaper, I would go to the entertainment section to get to know the names journalists. Most, if not all newspapers and online blogs portray the names of the writers of articles, so I would take screenshots or jot their names down.

I would then search these journalists on social media, send them private messages; greet and kindly request their emails and telephone numbers and letting them know why. For example, "Greetings Ms Nkosi, I am Colani Nkosi aka SooPurB, a Siswati Hip Hop musician from Mpumalanga. I would appreciate being featured on your publication as I'm currently promoting my new song. I kindly request your email address so I can forward my press kit." My press kit always includes the press release, press photos, profile and song download and streaming links.

The press release serves as the email body and the subject line can be 'ENTERTAINMENT NEWS.'

Greetings Press Release

Entertainment/Arts and Culture

16 APRIL 2030 (Put The Date On Which You're Sending It)

SOOPURB ENCOURAGES HUSTLERS NOT TO GIVE UP WITH A

NEW SONG - SKELEM (Headline must be informative and catchy).

After you've coined a catchy and explanatory headline for your press release, the next thing is to elaborate more. Your headline is just a skeleton of your press release so you must add meat to it. You can write it how you like as long as it briefly explains the song and it's content, what's the inspiration behind the record, featured artists etc.

Just like any e-mail, in the end, you put your contact details. Since you're an artist that's still striving to build and sell one's brand, make sure you include your social media links, handles (and/or usernames). Most publications have their social media pages and they might want to tag you, and that might help you gain followers.

Remember to call after sending your email because it might go straight to the recipient's spam folder. At times it can be delivered as you wish but the journalist will keep on serving those who make follow up calls. If you're scared to call, hire a PR or else you'll be the person always whining and claiming that the industry gatekeepers are closing doors on you when you haven't even knocked.

Chasing journalists and bloggers via DMs is not always gonna work, most of them are likely not to reply or you might text a wrong person with the same name and surname and that's so common on social media. So the most efficient, effective and convenient way to get a writer's email and contact number are to call their receptionist and tell them what you need, they'll help you...simple as that.

No matter who you're texting privately to ask for help in any industry or business, DO NOT waste time by saying 'Hi' and wait for a response, most people don't respond to that. Greet, give brief information about yourself and get straight to the reason you're texting, all at once. Be specific and straightforward. Say it all in one shot. You might miss a lifetime opportunity by trying to be chatty-chatty on DMs of people you want help from or wish to do business with.

CHAPTER 7

HOW TO EASILY GET OTHER TALENTS TO WORK WITH YOU

This chapter originates from what I usually experience when trying to work with other talents in which I saw potential and talents that initiate to work with me because they supposedly saw potential in me. When I started getting featured on various platforms such as radio, TV and papers most of which many artists wish to be featured on, my DMs, WhatsApp and phone got flooded by artists wanting to work with me on their projects.

Whenever an artist hit me up for some work, first I would evaluate the value that I'd be getting from working with him or her and then focus on their sounds, understanding of the music business and their track record. I wanted to avoid working with artists who are not as committed as I am because I didn't want to waste my energy and time writing and recording music that would possibly go nowhere. For me to agree to work with somebody, there must be synergy.

Since my main mission has been to expose my music and my brand to the masses, I intentionally choose to work with artists who got the same eagerness and energy as mine. Before I agree to work with another artist I first check if the collaboration will bring me value or something that can be beneficial to my brand.

If you hit up someone you wish to work with and you don't have money to pay for their services, determine what have and that they might need and propose to exchange services. Even before money existed people exchanged goods for goods. You give me a goat and I give you a sheep. Most of us aspiring artists are barely able to afford the expenses of the music business but we have a lot to offer in exchange for what we need. If you got nothing to offer the next person you want to work with, unfortunately, you got to pay.

I got plenty of artists who wanted to work with me for free and they had nothing valuable to offer and I turned them down. Artists saw that I got featured on certain platforms and they believed that working with me is a ticket to those platforms. Most of those artists didn't even bother to even listen to my music let alone knowing what genre I do. I appreciate their interest in working with me but their motives are just parasitic, they're just bloodsuckers and are not in any way going to benefit me so ain't no reason for me to waste my energy on such endeavours.

Let me share with you a short conversation I had with an artist on messenger. He wanted to feature me on his project and as usual, he didn't even try to check out my music. He just saw my Facebook profile, a photo of myself performing on YoTV and probably checked my other photos and saw that I've been on various media platforms, radio, TV, newspapers etc. And beside him wanting to work with me solely because of my profile, he was not bringing me any value and couldn't even communicate properly.

This is how the convo went:

Him: Awe

Me: Ola what you telling me?

Him: 8ta nix I just want you and me to work together on my album set to drop in April. Me: Sho, what kind of work do you wish to accomplish?

Him: Music bro

Me: Be specific man

Him: Ekse in April I want to drop an album so I want to work with you

Me: what is it exactly that you wish me to contribute, is it production? Pr, artworks or what?. If I wish to work with someone I specify like; I'm working on a song and I want to feature you...how much will you charge me? Or I'm working on a project and I need you to help with promoting.

Him: Oh what I want to say is I want to feature you on the album I want to drop in

April.

Me: Do you know the type of music I'm doing? Him: What kind of music do you do bro?

Me: Oh! Then why do you want me to be on your album because you don't even know the type of music I do? Are you even sure that I make music?

Him: Yes I'm sure that you do Hip Hop, RnB and Kwatio and that's the reason I want you on my album.

Me: Where did you get the assurance about the type of music I do because you don't know any of my songs?

Him: Eish! Ekse I forgot to ask you...sorry Me: Ever heard one of my songs?

Him: Nop

Me: So you want to put me in your album but you don't know if I'm good or not? Him: I will teach you

Me: Why don't you just get people you're sure are talented and work with them because you can't teach me to be a good artist by April?

Him: Aaah ekse I hear you, I'll look for others.

Me: I wish you nothing but the best in finding the best artists for your album but I still wish to know what is it that made you pick me and wish to have me on your album? Knowing your motive or reason behind wanting to put me on your Album might motivate and encourage me to work hard and become a better artist.

Him: Bye-bye ekse

From this conversation, you can tell that the artist simply wanted to work with me because he saw my YoTV performance photo and he thought working with me will benefit him. He didn't even bother to listen to my music so he doesn't know the genre and sound I do. So basically this artist doesn't know what he wants, he just wants to appear on TV and be famous that's all. Sadly that's not how it works.

This artist could not even state his reasons for wanting to feature me he was just being parasitic. For other artists to consider working with you, you got to present to them a mutually beneficial collaborative plan. If the collabo is meant to only benefits you, PAY UP. This is the type of guys who claim that certain artists are cocky, arrogant, big-headed and not easy to talk to.

You need to do thorough research of artists you want to work with, know their taste, style and everything there is to know about them. While you study an artist, you are likely to discover things they might need that you can easily be able to provide them with in exchange for their services, features, beats, engineering and more. For people to even consider working with you, they look for value. If you don't offer them something valuable, just pay.

One of the people I got to exchange services with is the youngster that produced most songs on my debut EP, his name is Ace Julz. I got to listen to his songs and I was amazed. He told me he makes his beats. Because I wanted his beats and I didn't have money, I offered to help him with PR, I got him a radio interview and we were good to go. Another guy, Da Saint came for my PR services and he proposed to offer beats and a feature in return and we worked. If their beats were bad, I wouldn't agree though.

In the music business, working with people is one thing you cannot run away from. Paying people for their services is something you got to do most of the times. Do you need beats? Buy. Do you need studio time? Pay for it. No matter the service you may need, you either have to part ways with money or offer something the other party might need. And don't be like the artist that initiated the convo above. Before you even dick ride, know at least the size of the dick.

No one in any kind of business would waste energy, time, effort and money on something they don't benefit from. It's called the music business for nothing. Before approaching artists for features, thoroughly prepare your pitch and be as professional as possible.

And as much as having a famous artist on your project will somehow benefit you, it also has disadvantages to be mindful of. Paying a big artist to be on your song doesn't mean he or she will help you promote the song. You can go all out tagging them on social media and not get even a single retweet or a share, let alone a post about your song from them.

Regardless of how popular the artist you featured is if he doesn't get involved in promoting it, it becomes obvious that he only did it for the money. Another disadvantage of featuring a big act is that they might overshadow you in your song, people can listen to only him and skip your part.

There's a lot of things to consider before you try to work with other people. Look at yourself, your level and check your sound as well as theirs and see if the two of you have commonalities. As upcoming artists, we need to accept the fact that for us to break into the game, we need to take the stairs, no shortcuts to the top.

Chasing well-known artists to get them to boost our careers is a shortcut that often doesn't yield good results. Let's put in work and not try to take advantage of other people's shine. Collabos are good for our careers but they should be natural, strategic and not forced.

CHAPTER 8

PROMOTING YOUR MUSIC AND BRAND ON SOCIAL MEDIA

Before the birth of social media, artists and brands depended only on traditional media (radio, TV and print) to get publicity for their music

and brands. Now we have various social media platforms you as an artist can use to your advantage.

The first thing that an artist needs to strategically execute is setting up social media names also known as usernames. Avoid setting up usernames or handles that don't that are too different from each other like being @ soopurb_king on Facebook, soopurb_sa on Instagram, @SooPurB_global on Twitter etc. For people to easily identify you on social media, try to use one or the same username across all these platforms.

Keep your social media username simple. My username on all my social media accounts is @SOOPURBTHEKING, though on it varies with the small letters and caps but the spelling is just ONE. On Facebook and Twitter, it's just @SooPurBtheking and on Instagram and Tiktok it's just small letters @soopurbtheking. However, one can search me on any platform using either caps, small letters or mixed and my account will show up regardless.

Most artists hardly remember to differentiate and spell out their social media names during interviews because they confuse themselves too. Even if they do remember them correctly, if their different, it will be difficult for a person listening to, for instance, their radio interview to grasp each unique name for each platform.

Since my username is same on all my pages, during interviews I simply say, "find me or follow me on all social media platforms as @ SOOPURBTHEKING...spell SooPurB as S Double O, P, U, R, B." This strategy will also help when, for instance, a person follows you on one platform, it will be easy for them to recognise and follow you if your username pops up on their other platforms.

If you're ABC this side and DEF on the other side, you're no different from someone skipping a country and forging a new identity. And people do such because they do not want to be identified nor recognised. As much as you want to look creative and unique, also employ simplicity.

Well-known artists such as A-Reece and Lil Wayne do use different usernames on social media even ones that aren't matching their stage names. For example, Lil Wayne is ''@LilTunechi'' on Twitter. A-Reece is ''@theboydoingdoingthings'' on Instagram and ''@reece_youngking'' on Twitter. Well, it works for them because they have millions of followers who know these "also known as" names of theirs.

Another thing to be mindful of especially when promoting a song or body of work is to refrain from posting the same artwork a million times. Use your phone to record short video clips of yourself singing the song, dancing to it, playing it in the studio and other types of creative promotional visuals.

Remember, people are on social media to socialise, so incorporate your music into socialising instead just pestering people by asking them to stream or download your song. While someone might enjoy watching you dance, they'll be inevitably listening to your song and they might like it and even want to cop it. Lately, songs become popular via Tiktok while people are having fun doing different types of comic challenges.

Instead of asking people to listen to your music, use other means to entice them, show your passion and talent through videos. Sometimes go live on Facebook, Instagram or any platform while you're in the studio making a song. Dj Tira starts promoting a song by going live while it's being made. People want entertainment and if you give it to them, they give you their attention.

Another big problem that makes people not take emerging artists serious is the use of language. The tone, grammar errors, choice of words and spellings have a huge impact on your social media marketing. Refrain from shortening words the same way we did on Mxit years ago. If you're not sure of the correct spelling, check a dictionary instead of writing 'dwnlod' 'frnd' '2day' and other unprofessional words. This is business so avoid looking incompetent at all costs.

Your friends might understand this type of broken writing but it's jargon to other people. Keep your captions, titles and language as professional as possible. Learn the basics of copywriting on the internet, YouTube or ask someone to help you draft nice and catchy captions. Also, watch and learn how your idols caption their posts.

Also, make use proper # tags on your social media posts to optimise your reach. Search for # tags that are related to what you post and also creatively come up with your own. One mistake that artists make is using # tags that are trending but not relevant to their posts. What does #NelsonMandela, #FeesMustFall have to do with your music? Be creative and strategic when using # tags and make sure they link with your content.

Most used # tags are more likely to extend your reach. Also do not overload your posts with # tags, choose the most relevant two or three and add one of your own, keep it short, sweet and straight to the point. Instagram even shows the number of posts that ever used a # tag. What you also need to avoid when dealing with # tags is to NOT go for the ones that have been used a million times because your posts will be lost in those millions and end up not being seen.

Also, don't make the mistake of ignoring and not interacting with the people who comment on your posts. Don't act like big artists who get thousands of comments and obviously can't able to react or respond to each person. You can reply to them all collectively with one comment and attend individually the few that need specific clarity or asking unique questions.

The more active you are on your social media platforms, the more your reach expands and followers grows. Even if you don't necessarily type your responses, you can use emojis or react to the comments. Be as friendly possible on social media, it's PR.

No matter how good and proper your music is, if your branding ain't professional, people will hardly be convinced to even try listening, they just won't take you seriously. The type of music you make, what you wear, the type of photos and videos you post all have a huge impact on your brand.

Whenever someone looks at any of your social media profiles, content you post, photos and videos as well as the captions, they must see a superstar ready for the limelight. Through your social media platforms, promoters, journalists, bloggers and the public at large must see a musician whose music deserves to be heard, a brand to work with, invest in, and performances worthy to be paid for.

The only way to achieve proper branding is to invest money, hours and energy in your work, do professional photoshoots, get your graphical content properly designed and videos properly shot and edited. Also, check social media pages of your idols, check how your favourite and successful artists do their thing and do like they do yet in your own creative and unique way, do not copy.

"Be yourself, everyone else is already taken." - Oscar Wilde

CHAPTER 9

INDEPENDENCE VS. BEING SIGNED

I get plenty of artists asking me plenty of questions about record labels and record deals. Artists envy fame, gilts and glamour and think it's on record labels that will make them famous and rich. They don't even take the initiative to do research and familiarise themselves with record deals and their advantages as well as disadvantages. With the existence of the internet and YouTube, one can get a full understanding of how record labels work in a matter of minutes.

When an artist signs a 360 record deal, all expenses are paid for by the record company and all the money must be recouped (paid back to the company) once the artist starts making money through gigs, record sales, merchandise sales, endorsement deals etc. Basically in such a deal, the artist is given an advance, which serves as capital (a loan) to kick-start his or her career.

As an artist, you only focus on making music. The business side of things is handled by the label. And in such a deal the music is owned by the label, not the artist. This means that you do not have control over the master recordings of the music you make. They spend money on you and once you blow they take it back and then share the profits after.

Also, in a 360 deal, an artist is obligated to record a certain number of albums or stay in the company for a specific period depending on the contract, and failure to do so has consequences. If you agree to make 3 albums before you opt-out or either sign that you'll spend 3 years in the company, you must do so or else serious legal actions are taken against you.

Some artists who leave record labels before contracts end, usually remain

inactive until the contract's term ends. Labels use such strict contracts because artists get pouched by other labels or decide to go independent once they got their breakthrough and leave the label in debts.

Most of the time artists sign 360 deals and once the money comes in through record sales, deals and gigs they feel like labels are robbing them and demand more money. Artists should know what is it exactly they are getting themselves into before they sign 360 deals to avoid regrets and financially exhausting legal battles.

Nowadays record labels do offer deals such as 'licensing' and 'distribution' deals. In a licensing deal, the artist finances their music production costs and the label starts promoting a finished product. Also, the artist owns their master recordings. Both parties, the label and the artist negotiate and agree on sharing the profit generated only by the licensed music. The artist will also manage itself, have a manager or management company of their choice. The label is also not having a share of the artist's other revenues.

In a licensing deal, the label only handles and take profits of the licensed music and not interfere with other businesses of the artist. Record labels, however, do not just give such deals to anybody. They do licensing deals with artists in which they see potential and the potentiality of return on investment. Most known indie artists sign such deals.

A distribution deal is mainly about getting a major label or a distribution company through which your music will be distributed to the public. The artist gets someone to sell their music and split the profit from record sales. Unlike all the other music business deals, a distribution deal is less complicated and easy to get, especially in this time and age whereby technology simplified almost everything.

Most artists are now able to work their way up to the top independently. They finance everything from their own pockets. The secret of succeeding in the music industry as an indie is to thoroughly study and know the industry. You must know people who make things happen. Though it's twice harder to make it independently, the rewards are splendid.

One way or the other you will have to get some people to help you and you must pay for most services. As an indie, you're your team and executive and the workload is all on your shoulders. It's possible but tough to make it on your own so you need to be informed about the business otherwise you won't win.

Whether you aim to be signed or going indie, you must be a hard-working artist. For record labels to notice you, your stuff must outstanding and your work ethic unmatched. No record label will dig you from the comfort of your home. You got to get out your comfort zone and start making moves.

And as much as you to get signed and make money, bear in mind that a label aims to make money through you and your talent. Of course, labels do help talents and change their lives, but do so with the sole purpose of making a profit.

As a signed artist, you're just like anybody employed by a company and they can be fired should they become unproductive or misbehave. Some artists work hard and after getting signed they start to relax and expect the label to do magic. Signed or not, you still need to work hard to achieve your goals and dreams.

CHAPTER 10

DESIRE, VISION AND FOCUS

The effort, seriousness and determination a person employs when chasing their dreams, stem from the desire he or she has. Just like a vehicle needs fuel to start and move from one place to another, a dreamer needs a strong desire to begin chasing their dream. The amount of fuel also determines how far the vehicle goes, just like the desire a person has determines how big they will win.

Artists quit schools (e.g. Cassper Nyovest) and 9 to 5 jobs (e.g. Touchline) to pursue their music career. There are things you must quit or sacrifices you must make in order to focus on winning in the music industry. In Mzansi artists relocate from their neighbourhoods to Jozi to chase their dreams and they are pushed by their desires. But don't quit school and head to Jozi without a plan claiming you got a strong desire you will end up in the streets.

Also have a vivid vision of where you wanna be, how you wanna get there and who or what you wanna become. Have mental pictures of your musical journey. Yes, you wish to be like Nasty C, AKA or whoever but you won't be their clones so you must have your vision. A vision serves as your map and navigator for your unique journey. Also make sure that the people you work with understand your vision or else your ship will hit an iceberg, break and sink.

No one can create a vision for you, it has to be self-created. All your plans, re-planning and actions will be informed by your vision. Your vision serves as the ground on which you lay the foundation of your music career, without one you won't achieving anything.

All the things I've mentioned and discussed in this book will only be accomplished if you focus and work on each one at a time. For instance, when you do your SAMRO registration, do it and finish before you move to RISA. Finish whatever job you start before starting a new one because you'll end up having many unfinished businesses.

Without focus buildings don't get built, paintings don't get painted, and time and energy get wasted. If you make music, focus only on it and finish and when it's time to promote your music, focus on it. Multitasking is a good thing but when you do major tasks it only results in mediocre outcomes.

No matter how good and informed your plan is, you will always come across challenges and setbacks. How you respond to problems and hiccups will determine your success or failure and this applies to any industry and business. Whenever you fail, make sure you learn so you succeed on the second attempt.

Most people are afraid to do things just because they fear failing. Successful people are those that are willing to fail, get rejected and face challenges and storms that come their way. Fear of failure is the enemy of success, don't be afraid to fail. Through failing you learn, grow, improve and succeed.

Link up with me on social media @SooPurBtheking

...

References www.samro.org.za[6] www.risa.org.za[7]

www.sampra.org.za[8] www.capasso.co.za[9]

6. http://www.samro.org.za/

7. http://www.risa.org.za/

8. http://www.sampra.org.za/

9. http://www.capasso.co.za/

About the Publisher

Mbokodo Publishers is your choice service provider and partner in the publishing business. We make your business our business in order to understand your needs, tastes and challenges better so we could provide you with the most efficient services imaginable.

Our professional and committed staff and personnel are always ready to assist you whenever you contact us. So drop us an email or simply call or visit our offices and this could be the beginning of a positive change in your life!

We look forward to being of ultimate assistance to you our dear prospective clients. For more information with regards to our offered products and services, please email us, mbokodopublishers@gmail.com

We look forward to hearing from you soon. God bless you!

Regards,

Publisher

www.ingramcontent.com/pod-product-compliance
Lightning Source LLC
LaVergne TN
LVHW050933080826
845145LV00004B/1249